SMOKE JUMPERS

extreme jobs

Sarah Tieck

Big Buddy BOOKS
Extreme Jobs

ABDO
Publishing Company

VISIT US AT
www.abdopublishing.com

Published by ABDO Publishing Company, 8000 West 78th Street, Edina, Minnesota 55439.

Copyright © 2012 by Abdo Consulting Group, Inc. International copyrights reserved in all countries. No part of this book may be reproduced in any form without written permission from the publisher. Big Buddy Books™ is a trademark and logo of ABDO Publishing Company.

Printed in the United States of America, North Mankato, Minnesota.
062011
092011

 PRINTED ON RECYCLED PAPER

Coordinating Series Editor: Rochelle Baltzer
Contributing Editors: Megan M. Gunderson, BreAnn Rumsch, Marcia Zappa
Graphic Design: Marcia Zappa
Cover Photograph: *Alamy*: All Canada Photos.
Interior Photographs/Illustrations: *Alamy*: aaron petersen.net (p. 17), All Canada Photos (p. 7); *AP Photo*: AP Photo (p. 25), Ric Francis (p. 11), Barry Gutierrez (p. 17), Gordon King/Yakima Herald-Republic (p. 19); *Bureau of Land Management* (p. 25); *Corbis*: ©Michael S. Yamashita (pp. 13, 27); *Getty Images*: Stephen Ferry/Liaison (p. 5), Tyler Stableford (p. 9), Justin Sullivan (pp. 7, 17, 23); *iStockphoto*: ©iStockphoto.com/jabejon (p. 30); *Photo Researchers, Inc.*: Ken M. Johns (p. 21); *Photolibrary*: Index Stock Imagery (p. 29), Peter Arnold Images (p. 15); *Shutterstock*: Galyna Andrushko (p. 30).

Library of Congress Cataloging-in-Publication Data

Tieck, Sarah, 1976-
  Smoke jumpers / Sarah Tieck.
    p. cm. -- (Extreme jobs)
  ISBN 978-1-61783-027-3
  1. Smokejumpers--Juvenile literature. 2. Wildfire fighters--Juvenile literature. 3. Smokejumping--Juvenile literature.
I. Title.
  SD421.23.T57 2012
  634.9'618--dc23
                      2011017450

CONTENTS

SMOKE JUMPING 101

Every year, fires destroy forests and other natural areas. Smoke jumpers are firefighters who work in places that are hard to reach. Smoke jumpers leap out of airplanes or helicopters to reach burning forests! They work to slow or stop fires. This extreme work is an important public service.

When smoke jumpers are needed, they put on their gear and head out. Fires spread quickly, so everyone moves fast!

UP IN SMOKE

Smoke jumpers fight fires deep in forests or high in mountains. There may be few or no roads in these areas.

It is hard for cars or trucks to quickly get to these fires. It is also hard to bring firefighting tools there. So, smoke jumpers fly in bringing much of what they need.

Smoke jumpers work in groups of 2 to 20 people. Each smoke jumper carries about 100 pounds (45 kg) of tools and gear.

FIGHTING FIRES

In the United States, most wildfires happen between June and October. During this time, smoke jumpers may live together at a jump base. When there is a fire, they go to work.

Smoke jumpers work in groups. They fly to the fire together. Then, they jump in pairs. They carry bags full of gear. After they land, other tools and supplies are dropped nearby.

FACT ALERT

Wildfires are most common during dry, warm weather.

Smoke jumpers carry their own gear. So, they prefer tools with more than one use. The Pulaski can be used as an ax and a hoe.

Smoke jumpers start by clearing areas in the fire's path. They cut down trees and dig out grass and other **debris**. These plants act as **fuel** for a fire. Removing them keeps the fire from spreading. This cleared-out area is called a firebreak.

WORK WEAR

Smoke jumpers wear strong jumpsuits to keep them safe when they jump. The jumpsuits are padded and very hard to rip. Smoke jumpers may also wear masks to help them breathe. And, special screens cover their faces.

A smoke jumper's parachute (PEHR-uh-shoot) is packed into a backpack. After jumping, the parachute unfolds to slow the fall. This lets the smoke jumper safely land on the ground.

A jumpsuit has pockets on the legs for storing gear.

After landing, smoke jumpers take off their jumpsuits. Under them, they wear clothes that don't catch fire easily. They put away their parachutes and jumpsuits. Then, they often put on hard hats and gloves to stay safe from fire.

A smoke jumper carries gear in a bag. This gear includes gloves, a hard hat, drinking water, food, and two-way radios.

GEARING UP

Smoke jumpers sometimes fight fires with water. But, water pumps and hoses are often not available. Instead, they use tools to slow or stop the fire's spread.

After smoke jumpers land, they get their tools. Chain saws help them clear branches and trees. They may dig up dried leaves and grasses with shovels or Pulaskis.

Two-way radios help smoke jumpers talk to each other.

Smoke jumpers carry rope in case they get caught in a tree after jumping. They can use the rope to lower themselves to the ground.

Planes help smoke jumpers from the air. They drop a red liquid called slurry on fires. Slurry helps slow the fire. Its red color shows where it has been dropped.

SAFETY FIRST

Sometimes fires get out of control fast. Smoke jumpers try to stay out of the way. But if they need to take cover, they go inside a fire shelter.

This shelter is made of special cloth. It can keep people safe in extreme heat for a short time. It folds up so a smoke jumper can carry it.

Smoke jumpers practice using fire shelters. They always carry them but only use them in a fire if they have no other choice.

COOLING DOWN

Smoke jumpers work hard and long to stop a fire. After the fire is out, there is still work to be done. Smoke jumpers must clean up the area. They carry tools, gear, and garbage out of the forest. This is called the pack-out.

After a forest burns, new trees grow again over time.

READY, SET, GO!

Smoke jumpers are specially trained firefighters. Many have a college **degree** in a science, such as fire science. They must first work for a time fighting wildfires. Then, they train to safely jump from an airplane.

Smoke jumpers practice jumping into different landscapes. They jump into areas with water, trees, and open spaces.

THEN TO NOW

The first smoke jumpers began fighting wildfires in 1940. Two people made the first jump.

Before this, firefighters called smoke chasers fought wildfires. They had to hike several days to reach deep forest fires. They were worn out before they even started to fight the fire!

Smoke jumpers have always used parachutes in their work.

Smoke jumpers were important during World War II. People wanted to be sure America's forests stayed safe. They were afraid enemies might attack this way.

FACT ALERT

World War II was a war fought in Europe, Asia, and Africa from 1939 to 1945.

Today, there are about 400 smoke jumpers in the United States. They work in groups to fight fires around the country.

Over the years, very few smoke jumpers have died. But, many have been hurt while jumping from planes.

BACK TO BASE

When they are not fighting wildfires, smoke jumpers keep busy by doing other work. Some may help with other forest jobs, such as collecting data for science. When wildfire season is over, many smoke jumpers have different jobs.

A smoke jumper's extreme job saves valued natural areas. This work is an important public service.

When they are not fighting fires, smoke jumpers may check parachutes for holes and fix them.

WHEN I GROW UP...

Explore parts of a smoke jumper's job now!

Smoke jumpers spend time in forests and other natural areas. Ask an adult to take you for a walk in a forest. Or, go camping!

Smoke jumpers must have strong arms, backs, and stomachs. They carry heavy tools and do lots of walking. You can eat right and exercise to grow strong and healthy.

Smoke jumpers often ride in helicopters or airplanes. Have you ever been in a plane or a helicopter? Ask an adult if you can plan a trip that includes flying!

IMPORTANT WORDS

debris (duh-BREE) bits and pieces of something broken down or wrecked.

degree a title given by a college, university, or trade school to its students for completing their studies.

fuel (FYOOL) something burned to give heat or power.

WEB SITES

To learn more about smoke jumpers, visit ABDO Publishing Company online. Web sites about smoke jumpers are featured on our Book Links page. These links are routinely monitored and updated to provide the most current information available.

www.abdopublishing.com

INDEX